LOOSE LEAVES FALL

Selected Poems

Kerry Shawn Keys

PINE PRESS
Camp Hill Pennsylvania
1977

FIRST EDITION

Manufactured in the United States of America
for the Pine Press, 3808 Chestnut Street,
Camp Hill, Pa., 17011

Typography by Batsch Co., Camp Hill, Pa. 17011

Library Of Congress Cataloging In Publication Data:

Keys, Kerry Shawn, 1946-
  Loose Leaves Fall.

  Poems.
  I. Title.

PS 3561. E94L6 811'.5'4 77-10170
ISBN 0-930502-00-0

ACKNOWLEDGEMENTS:

Some of these poems have appeared previously in
ICARUS, PRISM INTERNATIONAL, THE MICHIGAN QUARTERLY
REVIEW, STONEY LONESOME, EPOS, NORTHERN LIGHT and
THE MISSISSIPPI VALLEY REVIEW.

The first two sections are reprinted from
SWALLOWTAILS GATHER THESE STONES (Kanchenjunga
Press, 1973) and JADE WATER (Kanchenjunga Press, 1974).

CONTENTS

All matter is spent light . . . the luminous
turns to a prevalence of luminous, and this
prevalence turns to flame, and flame de-
teriorates into material, and material be-
comes means, the possibilities, the evidence.
So therefore mountains are spent light, the
streams are spent light, the air is spent
light. You are spent light. . .

Louis L. Kahn

These poems are gathered for

    Lewin
    Holy Man
    and Kernel Sess

Poems
from
Swallowtails
Gather These Stones
(1973)

DOWNWIND

A saltlick
Set back from the road
Marks a last outpost of bounty;

Downwind in the snow,
The eyes of a buck
Seal into whiteness.

What stalks,
Planted on a side ridge,
Is only a stump to him;

And what wheels
Overhead
In wide circles

And forecasts
Blood burning in,
Flake on flake,

The collapse of muscle,
The slow rip of belly,
The scarlet fruit,

Is no more than a shadow
Among shadows
In the blizzard of featherless birds.

NADA

to watch the birds break the cherries
is to break the cherries. . .

at nightfall when the dark birds sweep up the insects
you listen to their music

when the world disappears
no one will tell it

the silence will come to fill up this space
it has come

the birds will go breaking
they will break their cherries
they will break their insects

you will not listen
you are not listening

this space is too vast

Time bends like a wing on your sky

MY BOWMAN

When the eye was coaxed from its orbit
the bower stood
and fingered the bow

There one finds the emptiness proper
for filling

I told the bowman
the monkshood lies in the well
the well lies in the circle of darkness
there we can wimble out love

Deep that night I showed the bowman
the red-tipped landscape of love
I showed him the feathers where the brain takes flight
I showed him the nave of love
I opened the lid he lost himself
He lost himself in the passage of love
that bowman
that swift-arrowed one

Now he stands and fingers his bow
My prize bowman wedded in war with my blood

GAME

I took that man
And slit him blind
In the red bush.

      Love is a cold song.
      A knife in the wind
      Sings with the wind.

He smelled like fox
Under the claw
Of night's crisp air.

      Where is your lover?
      Is he in the woods,
      Dead in the woods?

He hunted me,
Yet I bagged him,
Oh, held him hard.

      Hard, and then rolled him
      Bare upon the ground.
      Oh, he sighed, Oh.

I kept his teeth
Around my neck
For dear love's sake.

      No teeth, but an ax
      Chopped out of his sleep.
      He'll scratch your door.

No! I asked him—
Tell me of time
Tell me the years.

      But he told you more.
      His blood was like salt
      On that last night.

Why did he come?
I couldn't stand it.
I pulled him in.

      When the hunter knocks,
      The stock of his gun
      Asks for your life.

Yes. And my notch
For his barrel—
He pressed me there.

      Where? Onto the ground.
      You gouged out the moon,
      Then stript his tongue.

I wanted it.
That wordless root,
Flush to my lap!

      You might have asked him
      What his business was—
      Dead in the dark.

I did. I did.
But he was dumb.
I had his heart.

              You killed him for that
              You killed him for that
              A lover's game?

A hunter's game
And I was trapped.
No man does that.

LANDSCAPE

No profit to be got,
Stone-hood hums through this city's
Make-shift rot like a distant saw.

Slivers of glass on beds of dead lovers
Reflect moonlight; the walls protest
The shadow of bare-pimpled backs.

Exhausted against these grey walls, cars
Groan and cough; a thousand stories up
Women pull pressed roses from mottle-sagged breasts.

Thumbs of amputees hinged to fuck-you crews
Pound the eyes of blue-born clots
To the underlid of the street.

Meanwhile, taking advantage of the landscape,
A mole works above ground, bristles
Past discarded gears and lungs, drags

The tongue of a child
Like a devil's-paintbrush
Toward his cavity in the earth's heart.

BLOOD MOON

The moon wears her cloak down the sky.
She is black and heavy like the nightthroat of a frog.
Crawling in the sea her basket churns with soft-breasted turtles
and round silver fish throbbing like cold coins.

She fishes for the barking of dogs.
Her throat is full of seaweed and poisonous snakes.
Morning-glories burst from her
like trumpets.

An osprey shot
in the rip of the tide
stares at her with the waxed eye
and stiff wings of death.
A man pauses with his sickle raised.
His daughter embraces
the nutbrown belly of the earth.
When night falls the moon will hang from her
like a frozen lip.

MADMAN IN THE BODYHOUSE

Seven long months
I sat in this chair and thought
How each day they daily wanted
My soul to put on a winding sheet
And attend the state that brought
My coveted expanse, my seaward gaze,
And I laughed;

But not so loudly
To persuade myself of an intended joke
Or as a point of defense,
But rather a summoning
Of the sublime ridiculousness
That my position held, and I
Declined to alter the dream
That kept me still

Bordering the realm of an eccentric past
Not pleasing to their inhabitants,
At the least, a scapegoat for acquired nobleness
Or for the moral of a fine story told
To keep the times in place, the effectance within,
The union yoked

Of an emblem so ancient, so sought?
That they made the fact proclaimed
More substantial than the human heart,
Or my heart to be exact
Some curious sediment apart from
Any feeling other than their own;
And after seven months alone, unmoved
They declared me missing the essence of things
Gone over, dead.

FOR JOHN AND GRACE

in the dusk
a bird falls through amber trees

a fish, its belly to the wind,
resolves in silver admiration

the fish and the bird are confidants

in corruption

the fish glances ashore
and drops
the bird, in a shriek of feathers,
lowers

the wounded

the wounded walked up
they carried bags

the bags carried screams
screams

one scream
escaped

the wounded ran in mute circles

couldn't it cry?
couldn't it bleed?

the bags from generation to generation
knew what to do
with escaped screams

they grabbed it
shook it
stuck it
in the wounded's mouth

THE FINGER

In her room
A finger on the bed

Requires no attention;
She found it

With no personality
To nail it into recognition,

Or, at least, to complete
The analog of a similar finger

That stared above her childhood
Bed, a gift of Saint Xavier.

Each morning
She lifts it with a gloved hand,

Balances it on her head,
And grins out the window.

THE PRINCE

He lived in a land
Where warts grew larger than mountains,
Where the honeybee always left his hive
At an indecent hour.
If women approached, his member
Shrunk to the size of a bean, no
All Souls' Night for him.
Plagues of flies were inevitable in his presence—
Citizens doubted whether anything could be saved—
Hoards of locusts swarmed from invisible volcanoes—
Wrigglers entered into the most sacred chambers—
Termites feasted on occupants petrified in brothels:

He prodded everything.
He dallied with the leech and listened
To the earthworm's sexual moan.
He followed the wind and set stones on its tracks.
Everyone feared him.
His eyes were cold coins in the morning sun;
His beard pollinated with clouds of dust.
Everywhere forests fumigated themselves for him.

He said he followed this fable:
       (a road to the center of long light
       in vacuo, light without light
       seven stairs past the burning bush
       angels orchestrating their wings
       blindness: u-lu-lu
       the ears, All)
He disappeared.

The night he returned the moon lifted his mirror and fled.
He was bewildered. He came to me,
His legs withered with age,
His body crisp with pure light.
My hand gripped his. We became companions—

I led him into bars that opened like bottled wounds
Where our tongues swirled reservoirs of golden beer,
We plunged through streets' steaming coves that flowed forever,
We discovered the butterfly singing in its scented corolla,
We tasted young girls whose breasts were candles
              burning up our lips,
And young boys whose bodies were fearful shadows in our mouths.
Our feet followed the trellis and its vines into choicest vats.
Cellars swallowed us, fields buried us in quintessential grain.
We went everywhere.

At length he left me,
His mouth open with desire, his last word
Scraping a message of echoes: deaththhhhhhh. . .
He was in a hurry he flew the street's dark corridor
And as I followed down his shrinking form
The night paled,
And I thought of Tithonus
Who was once beautiful and lived with the Gods.

HERE, AT THE WORLD'S END

In Spring when the marsh wren sang to us of love,
And the cardinals spent their red fire across the pines,
We never felt the sand's embrace, or the crack of time
Where shells curl in their seasong and die.
We loved and the world loved us.

Here, at the world's end: Winter.
Countless gulls dip to the waves.
Interlaced with rose and silk seaspray,
Sails skimming the ocean like wings of doves,
Night has thrown its irretrievable net.

Stars scatter their ashes
In silver spikes across the sky—
Ghost-rigged masts. Last logs of breath.

In the open moon
An ancient craft breaks water.
What we ignored, beckons.
It is the hour of the high seashadow;
A time for embarking.

Shrouded in the fragrant portal
Our own hearts propel the ship—
We find the sea touches us, flows nowhere,
And goes under.

HUMMINGBIRD OF ABSENCE

Hummingbird of absence, mistress of silence,
your thighs are like the limbs of love's sweet house,
in you, night's arrow breaks his flight.

With dawn, the mockingbird tells me how you tossed the night
in the pine's green pincers. Daughter of love! I slept
like a ghost in the moss; morning found me translucent, attending
the grass, the leaves, the rain.

In this time of great flights my arms are of stone.
I live alone with lust, in an air full of roses and doves
the honeysuckle is my friend—the path you burn to me recurs
like some soul's dark migration, love spinning sightless
and home to my breast.

Your long beak and longer tongue
slip in and out of my dreams like rhododendron.

I want you! swift-feather star! I want you.
I am like a wounded bee who waits for the hour
of his love to blossom. Flower in wings, Fragrant bird!

Even in your nest your amber wings cut the air.
You are so far away. Ah, cup of forgetfulness,
night's fire, honey's golden thief, gather me
as the forest floor gathers the windswept pollen.
My songs, my words, shatter
before the pure lyre of your wings.

Sparrows bathing in the dust. Summer's pollen departs
like fine flour.
The bee's hum is lost in the cicada's shrill voice.
My passion builds a distant storm, clouds that overflow,
that bring you home,
petals that rain like flower chains on the mountain springs.

When you come, sweet bird, when you come,
our love will find the shape of the pine's sharp dust.
Moist and dark. Flower's fire.
We will fill everything. We will fill everything.

ALONG THIS RIVER, DELAWARE

In the water the lunar branches deepen
the earth is dying.
Often I feel myself fill with the sea
gently it comes,
then we roll over
mutable

What goddess lifts your breasts
forms the curves that shore this flesh:
Night says
it is the time of Honey
that gulls fly East lust on their wings

Along this river, Delaware,
memory strokes the quiet—
the fish stare ingathered
cold fins cutting the Chesapeake

Tonight we take them our sex—
this bed of moon and salt
these gestures steeped with words,
with limbs

WHAT DO DEAD SWALLOWTAILS DO

what do dead swallowtails do at night
do they sit in trees
like souls
and watch
the termites strip the wood

are they sempiternal Homoiousians
with breasts like stars
and members like swords

timeless
can they scent
corpuscles in the ground
or dead flies fall dead in piles of dung

these post mortems
leave many stones unturned

at night
the swallowtails gather these stones
and fly away

Poems
from
Jade Water
(1974)

BODIES OF SALT AND DEATH

The hourglass flows inward
to sand. Time, bowed incense-man,
his feet covered with barnacles and waves,
refuses to burn
his rose of stone. What blood,
which mask
split fine down the breastbone
will fold him upward
like some birdmoon
hunched
in a leafless night.

My mouth is his grave—
it swallows all the earth, myself
into toothless smoke. Webs draw over the eyes
and bind the blood away.
Are you dead? the moon snagged
to your thick stomach
like a crusted anchor, a calculus of lead
in the river's ebbing mouth.

O bodies of salt and death,
go away, go away, slag heap
on my heart's cold ash. Go away.
Grass fires, green fires, old man, sea fires!
burn these scabbed sheets, these nightfeeders
from my bed. Close on their leeching tongues
your sun that closes over water.
Sear them with your stars that fire
the vast dead coal of moonless nights.
Forge from their stones of gall,
from their brackish pale lips,
O forge for my heart a bloody rose of iron.

ROUND THE TOWER

through your breasts the roots dredge deep
they are hungry for the sea
they are tired with the squeeze of red fingers
they are tired of the cat in the throat
they want the darkest kiss
they want the angel stript
and the shaft of the moon
in his heart

on the wind lies a greenbird
by the sea floats a golden fish
round the tower
round the tower of the shaft in the moon
the cat will run   the cat will run
seeking the greenbird   seeking the golden fish

LORDS AND INCENSE

When I awoke that evening
a hazel rod was resourcefully tapping
the roots of my confinement; perfumed
in oceans of sweat, and disfigured by the imprint
plaited on my bed, I stumbled upstairs, unkempt and unveiled
like the naked host in his bakehouse.
My flesh stretched into parchment,
and my feet were coated with crossroads, garlic, and thorns.
I suspected that the Curators of Knowledge,
with all their stored light,
has gravitated to my home
and would rush
to meet me
if I opened the green shutters or pulled a blind.
I envisioned them outside
flashing their enlightened pommels of seeds and war,
swarming metallic hornets with diurnal heads
clanging clear like bells.
It was too much. I stole away,
retracing my measurements down the staircase,
and hiding
under the covers,
a steaming cowardly carcass.
For three days I survived,
extracting protein from pillowed chicken feathers,
and toasting, in semi-darkness,
alcoholic concoctions of an overactive yeast.
Three days of fundamental misery and bedsore atrophy;
three days tamped in my cell, a swollen termite,
my rods out of whack and crossbones outside the door.
Three days,

then suddenly benighted, a plan coalesced,
the spring welled to a brainstorm, and quickly
and obediently I removed my parts,
piecemeal by piecemeal:
shoving my head in a yellow baseball cap,
my feet in a pair of maroon argyle socks,
setting my trunk in a Hong Kong tailored suit,
my hands in a galvanized bucket of hot symbolic water,
and sandblind, this time when they knocked
the ground unlatched, and in slanted a blue light,
angelic badges and golden search warrants
beaming like torches fixed in deadfall hands—
Enshrined with incense and pennyroyal,
I waited on them in familiar fashion. . .
disconnected,
invisibly ultra-violet,
deadly
absurd,
before their naked, believing eyes.

BLOOD-BLADE

Blood-blade hone in the heart's vented home
Where your harpies swoop the huge reptilian sky
Their greybird metallic dagger tied taut
In the canary's trimmed incessant laughter—
There begotten fixed pitched forth with horny dice
They cast you this vise of bones and blood and flesh
These pressing jaws This procrustean madness.

GREENCASTLE

Exiles in the green castle,
all day the men and women
throw wounds over their children's heads.
All night, filled with emptiness,
they mold in the stony forests; enemies
of the mountain gorge, of deep rivers,
their breasts and groins fester
like stagnant, blighted moats.
Enemies of light, they fence
the glowworm's luminescence. Enemies of fire,
their embers entrench where the wing-case
veers into darkness.
Shoaled in granite on their mountain homes,
atolls of pumice far from the sea,
they feed on flowers like horseflies,
mandibles fixing blood to bones
cased like diatoms in cold backwater closets.
Silently their frozen tongues are icicles
pruning thighs, drawing pitch from bark.
And their children, damned, turn on themselves
forever, their lives weaved over,
returning to the rock they never left,
their white-banded lines like agates
marching into wood and space.

FIRE

Without flint,
without sun,
fire found the worm's highway,
grooved out the blood-channel,
bellowed the heartsmith,
scorched the flesh
into light. Light out of light,
fire in fire, dusked were the eyes of men
full of fire, the salamander
emblazoned his ashes
under rock.

Now fire
from the fallen fireman's glove,
fire in the palm of his hand;
fire in the wood,
in the seed, the ash. Fire
around the curtain's tail. Fire
where the hellbender
circles the river's mouth. Fire
hissing from its book.
Fire in the reed,
fire in the thief's throat,
in the giant's eye,
on the bird's beak; fire
when firestone flows,
fire behind the firewall,
fire where the dwarfed amphibian burns,
fire where his flaming tongue
eats through the blood's blue asbestos.

CANTICLE, THE GREY RETURN

Beneath the moon's basaltic path, the worm
waves an invisible spot of dark blood,
ice-tongs tearing at the granite maze.

The man himself or the worm
drifts through retreating forms,
formless under aeons of eternal light,

the blue smoke of earth a parallax
carved behind the eye, his blue socket
measuring a column of lava

colder than stars cutting through stone.
A gray snake of light climbs the frost-line,
calling his death a fissure in oceans of ice—

A detailed path: stone polyp in the foliage,
coral concealed between tongs of fire,
the anvil already blasting his winter lime. . .

what worm fathoms the outstretched zones, or
the man himself falling, falling, crosshairs of death
displacing every move,

deep-sea, deeper, the man himself
or the worm arcs under the frosted bow,
turning the crystal-lathe,

the lunar rotation, the grey return,
his furrowed lymph, protozoa of an incurved well,
marine, heavenly, futile.

NORTHERN LIGHTS

Snowmen brought the winterkill of wheat,
brown splintered ice from polar floe,
daylight eclipsed by the earth's long shadow,
cold winds at night and teeth upon ice.
Snowflakes fell like swandown torn to song,
all night, the springwood, winterbourne.

Out of the sea rose Botticelli's gift,
froth spun from a burning star,
salt-rime or hoarfrost, unseen,
untaken, less sea than wind.

Pine sap choked with seaweed, ambergris, no man
to yield the sign, to find the form from ice.
No man to warm the goddess in his bed. No eye
unbent for violets under the vine.

Old salts have all the facts nailed down:

From snow, men carved a winter shell,
snowmen working till they thawed in the sun.
Then, eager for love's kill, the winter-wind,
teeth lined with frost, the pack of the wind,
drove the goddess to the coffined boat.
There, shiftless with space, the impassioned star,
imprisoned in polar arms of the night,
drifts down the black light's long spiral claw.

ORION

Belted by the zodiac, the hunter's
cold sword thrashes in its clouded net.
Orion is dead, frozen grey to the gills,
and the world twists under
                              the scorpion's sting.

The hunter is dead, the lover. Now evil
conducts with pincered hands, peaceful
and unopposed.
And rust covers the giant's sword, fertilizer
for roses. All roses are blood's roses,
greenhoused in the neon sphere; all men
turn blue, then die for air.
Like the circles they were wreathed around,
dead roses erode through the living's blood;
and the Gods, starved in their wisdom,
ride out the concert into chaos.

Orion,
mortal and immortal have vanquished your sword,
they have killed and buried your blade
in the house for the dead.
Orion, Orion,
the scorpion whets his fire
in the sand.
Orion,
men are born green,
then die. Mice eat their bones.

MAIL POET POUCH TOBACCO

Women bound by the spell of words,
their tongues fall out of their breasts.
They wrap scrotums to death; grips
stronger than hemp. Scratched in a dark room
their wares flash like chromed tail-fins.

I ate crayfish once; night-strung women
with sharp bony jaws, turtles, no teeth.
Underneath—mining tools, their molted
lips teemed with surface film. O,
I wanted them all, front feet long
like rakes, bodies stiff under any shrub
in the garden. To browse over love.
Fine legs tapered to potholes. Eyes,
where drills could dig out the pupils.
Fingers at night to type on my back.

Lovers who eat these words
will climb into the cold like caterpillars
frozen to pines in late frost.
You, who read this, bait hooks with your lips,
will find moonworts uplifted by parables of pinafored sons,
cockroaches like upturned cars in your ovens,
dead poems in the salt-box, bygrade vitals,
maggots crawling like skirts with summer,
Greek-ripe olives for eyes,
Plucked!
BEWARE OF POET: crashed down in bitter grass
                    a bear salvaged his brain for junk
                    a muskrat hollowed out his ass
                    John and Jack dismembered his trunk
                    Mole refills his glass.

REQUEST

at evening
when the last leaf
turns from its tree—
take my heart to the forest
where the cicadas puncture the night

in the still morning
when the new moon drops
to its branch in the West—
bear my soul to the white river
where shad rush over the rapids

when the last leaf drops and the new moon turns—
carry me down
where the earth unfolds
where the moonflowers curl in the wind

LIME AND SLEEP

Love, it's a long way down this blue forest
of brine, this marbled matrix of lime
and sleep, where only the heaviest light
finds bottom.
Wings sweep over the breakers; white horses of foam.
I lie here at evening, alone, when the sea's dust
is rose quartz clustered with stars.
And I think of the mouthless silence, wave after wave
drowned as the sea tide remains, and the sea
remains the same masked vessel of blue light.
And who, in the last light, will sleep longer?
the sea, ten million years,
when it pounds and dreams for fire to chisel
lava from its bone; or the heart without sound,
the still body rolled out in the feral night,
lost abalone, wordless shell, staying
my love, for your hands' warm colors
to dress it to fire and stone.

COLD SUN

Winter, at dusk
the stars climb
through their arms
in the oak.
Firewood seeds
its heat
beside the road,
pine smoke, pine needles
thicken the air—
all that, all that.
My bed is fletched with frost,
sleep and frost,
yellow leaves around her hair;
the heavens dip their water in the stream,
the earth floats toward night,
every evening I ride this same sun
down into light.

MARRIAGE

Behind the arrowhead
that bites through bark,
the true snake
strikes flint
in the dark sweetfern.

Under the creek,
and yellow leaf,
the strange stick,
and smooth stone,
ancient druid bones
turn in their sleep.

Subterranean
their night-rivers
nightly meet.
Staff weds with arrow
and quivers
in its bow.
And heart!
O heart, my arm is bent
to ply your craft
their way.

SPRING

early May,
Donkeys bray,
Lynx-eyes
gleam from the Brush—
Bulls on Meadows
of Lust,
Men and Women
turn in Dust,
the Dust has them,
the Earth,
Laughter, Mirth

OUTSIDE THE WESTERN GATE

Under the rosetrees
at the equinoctial hour,
down where the snowflowers
spring from their roots,
there, my little wilding,
the ginseng and the anemone
are lifting their soft rays
through the oak
and the hemlock.

It is dawn,
little almond eyes,
and I am singing you
our watersong:

The stars have left
a fragrance
that stays,
and we stay, love,
outside the western gate,
though the sky
is scattered with blue
in its first turning light.

The greenbrier climbs
close on the laurel,
my heart's erect flint
blazes
like touchwood
on your breasts, two flowering quinces
on my lips,
two quail
quivering
in the brush.

All day
our hidden body
burns like an unmined
opal
on fire,
a cresset of kisses
untouched
by the sun's angry heat.

And when evening
opens
its cold mouth,
and the winds
whorl
into the wood
and into the lovers
that would embrace,
we knot our limbs
and our roots,
our tongues
and our blood,
and
endless and everywhere,
a five-petalled star,
all night
we burn
them
our brightest flesh.

Loose Leaves Fall
(1977)

LOOSE LEAVES FALL

LOOSE

    LEAVES

  FALL

FLYWAY

That breaks,
upended
breaks the flyway,
the trail patched with slag—
blue against amber wings
wedged into earth
like broken grass, broken grass.
To inscribe.
Again I hear the falcon
still turning the wind,
and I ask these grey stones
for a word
to hold a first feather
against the sun, the deep light,
the surviving snow.

A METHODOLOGY

Bipedal, under the worm-eaten sign
marked Greenwich, of unsound mind
and alone, I stand at my window
eating a mango, and watch the spiders at sea.
I stand at my window
and watch them watch me.

Sometimes I think they are dead starfish
trying to reform themselves for land.
Sometimes I let them dance on my tongue
while I tap a fingerbone.

Once I heard a butterfly say
after so many stories of flowers
that, in truth, it was in piss
that he rejoiced the most.
That in truth it was. . .

wasn't clearcut; there was a lesion
but it was a result of love
(the dead are like leaves in the forest).

If it is a matter of longitude and latitude,
celestial or mundane,
there is the North Mountain, the South Mountain,
the mountains to the East, and the red sun.

Or if this window serves as the point of departure,
then say it was my window on the world,
though the arc went counter-clockwise.
I had no way of seeing the spiders, or the stars,
except by standing up.

QUAYFEVER

Cunts and cobwebs, celestial
orangutangs and oranges,
covenants of inland ghosts
caulk the poet's hold on life—but now and then
with eyes half-shut with limestone
and colored like the setting sun,
he dreams himself wrapped in kelp
floating through breakwaters
of other worlds.
          Predators arrive:
a scallop with a ninth mutant eye
stalks the sinking wake; anchovies
assess his verses' protein count
against cargoes of soybeans and chalk;
a grunt deserts her wharfside bed
and sniffs the bloating bag of fruit.
          And now look—
the poet turns in his passage
like a giant prune fearful of too much water,
and dreams himself the other way,
low tide in the lee side of his withdrawing death.
          Still harassed,
a unicorn contends with a narwhal
for the bard's beached pelvic bone; spiders
cross his ankles with beards of sand,
and he finds himself stuck
in a delta of fibers, a network
of fishhooks, horseshoe crabs,
and the long arms of stranded jellyfish.

Poor poet!
hanging fire on the sea's edge,
the ocean grazes once again toward land,
the changing of the maritime guard;
and inbetween the particles
of water and sand, secret oysters,
that grind the moon all night,
rise in the longshore currents
to forage for his retreating form,
which crawls perpendicular and solitary
in the beachgrass, picking out
the star without a name.

SUN

In the clear stream
the sun, with iridescent arrows,
strips the trapped reflection of the alders
on the sand and rocks.
Like fish on fire
red anthers leap and cut my thighs,
and the shadow of the wind
hollows a dark rose in my groin.
But the heat here echoes
the hot pistil of the sun. Naked, I feel
the ferns unroll a secret fuel—the quarter moon,
hard coal, glows
in an emerald of fronds.
The small wind cries out as the moss
steams upward in the noonlight,
as my blood stiffens in heat.
Laurel and rhododendron surround me
with a bitter greenness; the air
arches before their hungry tongues.
They know my cock burns past them
toward the sun.

NARCISSUS OF HIS SHADOW

At summer's end,
by a long, low river,
my shadow was my lover.

She whispered of cherries
in the fallen oak leaves.
Her breath broke the soft blue grass
into a thousand crystals.

Amethyst and cool lights
from the earth, her eyes
grew drunk like small rowboats
loaded with lanterns and fish.

Her voice cut the hours
into clear harvests of bells,
'and her lips touched mine
like water-lilies, like wine.

On the riverbank, my shadow
pressed the new moon
deep in my breast.
With a kiss she stole me
to the dark entrance
of my own silhouette.

An old bullfrog croaked wildly
from the bitter watercress.

At summer's end,
by a long, low river,
my sister was my lover.
Her eyes were green lanterns
full of rowboats and fish.

HEART'S JOURNEY

Always the pollen in the rock,
I've kept the crystal there,
there, half-way there,
still deep in the stone's grain. . .
but a slow retreat to the heart,
and light relinguishes the spirit.

In the underleaf, a lacuna of silence,
the substitution of the pulse, the bloodheat,
for the caliper, the bright lattice
of the sun.

A moth under the hood of night
secures its ash
in the candle's extinguished light.
So my heart, when it shuts down at last,
will search the dark veined chrysalis,
and there, lame from the light,
flow wingless into the white circle
of the moon, that heavenly sea,
and rest in a kingdom of minerals,
unheard, unanswerable, under millennia
of brine-starred and flowering debris.

SANTIAGO

Night by night, all the skeletons rise from their grief.
Cool nights, and the water flows out of Acheron, out of
the heavy breath of the living . . . City!   Stars are cut,
turn, to smoke; umbrellas blow in the corners of streets . . .
black umbrellas, in the rain.
The Rain . . . and man?   Man.   O little one, small bride,
and they were herded into the stadium . . . reconstructed . . . great
gladiators, O little bride, widower in the closet. In your
hand, in your hands, the ring slips down his neck.   Man.   Turn
away . . . there's no song at the end.
The City, alone.   Black water, black water.
The Poet, dead. the heart, immense, immense! flaccid, collapsed,
Allende—bullet in his mouth, bullet in his mouth—bullet in his
mouth.
Dead. Chop wood.
Silence, between being and not-being, the pulse, at rest. . .
Into exile, all the shores, day into night.   Night lashed
to the lips of the storm.   Alone.
No measure.   No measure.   A black stone under the bed.
Blood in the widow's milk. . .
Umbrellas beaten by the wind.   Unrecalled, sleep.
the poet . . . the city . . . man.
Dead.   Chop wood.

THE MESSAGE

Pigeons are delivering shoes in the dark.
One lands on the roof all wrinkled with smoke.
Another, yellow with fear, shits on my heart.
They cry in shrill pigeon unison, "Kerry,
this is no time for love, no time for love."

O, the pigeons are delivering terrible shoes
in the dark.
I tell them, "Wait until morning, then I will come."
But their message is urgent,
It starts to unlace.
O, what terrible shoes the pigeons have brought.

I try to buy time; I tell them again,
"My hands are bankrupt, the moon is unmilked."

O, the terrible pigeons, they won't let up.

They scream that though I ride with you
on the ripest river of love,
a roadway of red lilies and fish,
that your kisses are lethal arrows
repeating themselves in my thigh's torn flesh
(The pigeons' eyes are clouded, syphilitic.
They have no heart. Won't be bought),
that our rapid dream is the poisoned word
of worms and wineburned doves.
They are running shoes in the dark:
make a poem like a stone for a neck
make a poem to cut a throat with
make a poem like a cross.

Love. And city of love, Rio,
vanished river of summer—
the stars are like small bonfires on your hills,
the skins of your drums tighter than anger.
I am afraid of morning, of the shoes by the bed,
of the unburied, necessary taste of love, its ocean,
of what the pigeons have said, of the cankers of the poor,
and of the demands that have been justly commissioned
by their unjustly dead.

THE GIRLS OF LAPA

The girls stitched
to the corner of morning
are Maria, Ana, and Cristina.
Their breasts are as sweet as mangos
and heavy like the rain at dawn.
Each carries under her dress
a red wound like the mouth of a fish.

Iemanja, take care of them—
Ana, Maria, and Cristina—
they bring you the clear sun of the grape,
and white roses whose thorns
they carefully break each night.

FIREWATER

What are words, or the hammered
sounds of the soul
spinning alone on its emery wheel
when I enter your torrid zone,
when I grind the dark home
of your sexual well, love, and like a rootless
star, fallen into night,
ride your phosphorescent and pelagic water
beyond these stony fields of silence
into coralline and nocturnal seas.
You are a coiled bird, a green dugout
set in the sea's growing crystal;
Quetzal, serpentine, fledging tiara of waves,
I drive again and again into the stormy salt
of your seawater, into your scarlet bay,
my breathing a groundswell of knives and stones,
our veins bursting with crosswinds of clay and milt,
our blood transforming the archives of the frightened earth.
And I fill you over and over with fire, your liquid undulations,
your feathered water, with fire
hurling a maelstrom of whitecapped and angry diamonds,
biting your breasts into bloodstones, tight
plumed insignias like incandescent comets
threading the moist night.
O lover, you are like a boat hollowed by a branch of fire,
I'll ride you all night, my slender seamare,
your nest saddled with hornets in heat,
my sperm racing through you like a lake of lava,
a blade of liquid fire,
the harsh kiss of our bodies
scorching the earth and the sun.

THE BRIDE

In the bride
the bronze, humped moon
opens like an instar,
closes like mountain water closing in
the water-hyacinth's feathers.

In her the sunflower
returns roots of light to earth,
anthers of fire into sap and marrow.

The bride is the mother
of the whippoorwill-hour,
the alembic, the worm's lover;
she is the lynx in the laurel
and the leopard's laurel tongue.

Bloodstone, stone-root, bloodroot,
of the bride's distinguished boarders
leap the lead-bullet,
the lizard's lambent tail,
Lupus and Lepus, Lumen and Lux.

Leaps Logos in flux germed in a loincloth.

She is the watershed and the skin just shed,
every image about to moult
and the image mortmained in the image about to moult,
the self, the herself and the himself,
the molten phoenix
                 manifest
                          in its copper matrix,
the empty nest.

FIRST MOVEMENT

(for Kyung-Sook Yu)

Unless you ignore this hand,
or this, or this,
all huddled in time,
you won't understand me.
For hands or flesh
are never enough
to catch the movement
that eyes can't grasp, the vision
that alters itself endlessly—
time, time, time
and again. Singer!
your ears are overwhelmed
by too much sound, the scent of roses
flies endlessly away in the night.
It is not the taste of things, somehow,
that makes them whole,
but the brief moment
when they reach out to touch
the soul's hunger and then escape you
like a chord moving from the tongue
as the soft vibration of the calloused thumb
lifts the unstrung guitar.

strifghtydf

occ   fghu dskjd   hjhj

agri   agripina anonima

agripa anonima

ghysdter   almeoths

rumos entr

Vila Isabel, Rio, August 13, 1976

ARCTIC MUSEUM

There is a heavy insistence
to the Earth. Wingless brown birds,
stars without centers, groundless atmospheres
move into her—mastodons,
whales, leviathans
greasing up the axlewheel.
Gnomic bones, half-human,
caught in her circle,
take shape without hope, greyness
from everything.

And their intention has always been this:
to breed extinction
like fusion. To work a way
into everything
and disappear—
stems into darkness.

Carcasses of light
bedded everywhere. But here,
hands pin them
under the sign of the Bear, encase
their geometries under snow.
And though desire
says yes and yes
to flow over, to cross,
this blue ice, cold fire,
preserves decay
forever.

JASPER

Jasper, hidden fire
of stone, layered pillar.
Of twelve
you were chosen
for the walls of brilliance.
They polished you,
rubbed the ruddy dust
from your surface
with hands almost blind.
Jasper, is it true
that you find in this New Jerusalem
that you were like an opaque sponge
for our blood,
and that your beauty
took from in us
the hard interior
of our own salvation.

COFFEE

This is where the nervecase breaks down:
cyclone of the second skin
where the bean unturns its spirit. Caffeine,
unwanted ghost of the wind. Wanted
where the synapse goes haywire,
sinks into the blood.
Where the *good berry* goes down.

Dead civilizations, on the edge of heat,
were unaware of its existence.
Too bad! Goats and sheep
awake all night in Ethiopia.

An aroma darker
than the Devil's stomach, black.
And when resting
under the mouth's roof, around
the tongue or in the throat—
bitter like hot sperm
or poet's ink.
Better swallow it quickly!

"At the base of the blossom
the dark berry develops."
Earth's blood. The darkness
of the berry
ripens her juice. Forbidden.
Unless roasted
and poured directly
into the open vein. Or sucked up
where the blood presses
its odyssey
hard on the brain.

BRINGHURST AORIST

The obscurity of his words
is their anthelion depth: the sun's pulse
under the earth, the toad's opposing shadow
in the moon, the rabbit's pale lip.
And a strange knowledge moves
under their white light—
the emerald uncut, fertile
in the uncarved block, the abrasive wind
in the hurricane's eye, the rapid
flow of blood in the riverbed
before the channel is cut.

Of the context: silence lifting, chromatic,
disappearing from the syllables,
reappearing:
the panther's breath
crouched in a cold mist
above the stars.

SEAWORM

Seaworm, brother,
isotope of celestial clay,
oblong, segmented ruin,
fallen Angel,
how long will you bore
through the liquid night,
disconnected, rapacious cipher
broken from the arrow's solar spine,
a black tunnel of emptiness
swallowing
rocks, circles, trees,
constricting all of Earth
and Heaven,
all my light,
breath by breath.

ON THE BANK AT TWILIGHT

(for my father)

As the light aligns itself
with the still lake,
bass begin to leap.
A time neither day nor night.

I fish in that light.
Once I found in the blue guts
of a large, black bass,
a black root
resembling a vein;

my Father taught me
to eat what I caught—but now
there are some things, some things
so mixed with chaos and pain
that (forgive me to be mad)
I always throw them back.

LAST SUPPER

That gray buzzard there on the limb
is my dead father, surely it's him
looking at me as I look back,
and both of us know this fact:

shared carrion, spade's spade, the hole's ace
is the coward fowl kept well-fed
in my inside's backyard instead
of here, now, lean, trussed tight to space.

IMPARTIAL POEM

Take flesh or take bone,
or whatever you often are
(if the moon, your heart from the moon)
out of context. Like blood
when it runs from a vein
and suddenly feels lost.
Take these things, take them
and your soul's compass deadlocks.
Take out the intimate things:
remove the red poem, the demons,
the women, the sun, so on,
then your clothes, then yourself.
What stays remains everything.
What remains stays a steel axis.
Or at times an impartial crystal.
It doesn't bend (light perhaps?),
or turn (colors like a prism),
or make itself or what is left
or what went (you) significant.
But it does speak, pronounces
what it wants, makes in otherwords
this whole universe, then takes
back everything, and you
with it, into itself.

THE LIZARD'S TAIL

Because the tail of the lizard
is drunk with rum and cumin
it likes to dance.
If it saw the undressed moon
shaving its profile
with a long fingerbone,
or heard the listless ants
picking its body
like an unwrapped snail,

where, in this world of buried light,
would it run and hide?

Because the tail of the lizard
is full of cumin and rum
it dances every night
until its shadow is gone.

But a man, lost, cut off
from the rhythms of earth,
has no choice but a task:

to find the dancing tail
and with it, step by step,
trace the one word
on the rubber lips
of the lizard, at dawn.